GET REAL!

GIRLS SPEAK

OUT ABOUT

EVERYTHING

GET REAL!

GIRLS SPEAK
OUT ABOUT
EVERYTHING

by Lori Stacy

all about **YOU!**

SCHOLASTIC INC.
New York Toronto London Auckland Sydney
Mexico City New Delhi Hong Kong

Special thanks to:

Alexa Piggott and Katherine and Kareline Moore
for their help with the surveys. Susan DerKazarian
for her patience and all her extra effort on *Get
Real*. And thanks, especially, to all the girls who
made this book possible by sharing their
thoughts, opinions, and even some of
their secrets!

Contents

Introduction

A Book About You

Imagine a get-together with your closest friends — talking, sharing secrets, and revealing your deepest thoughts and feelings. Now multiply that by over 50 girls and what do you get? *Get Real!* — a book that gets to the heart of what it's like to be a girl today.

Get Real! is truly all about you because it's written *by* girls like you. Girls from everywhere got in on the action and filled out our survey. We heard from girls from Alaska to Florida who were anxious to share their thoughts, feelings, hopes, and dreams.

What are girls today all about? According to the surveys we received, girls today are fun, optimistic, and outgoing, with a world of opportunity in front of them! Most of all, each girl we heard from is unique. What rocks one girl's world may be no big deal to another. While there's no way to learn about all of the things that make girls like you who they are, or to have heard from all of you, this book provides a look into what some of you had to say about yourselves. See if you recognize yourself in these girls' responses. How are you like them? How are you different?

How we did it: In June 1999, we sent out 500 surveys to a randomly selected group of *All About You* magazine subscribers from all across the USA. We received completed surveys back from 11% of the girls we sent them to — that is to say, from 55 girls. These girls served as correspondents for you. The ages of our respondents ranged from 10 to 15, with 13 being the average age. We've printed the survey at the back of the book so you can check out exactly what the questions were that the girls answered.

Chapter One

You and Your World

"In 15 years, I see myself being a masseuse in Tulsa, Oklahoma, with a husband, three children, and a small ranch house."
— **Jacqui,** 13, Plymouth, Wisconsin

"I see myself having a career — maybe on Broadway, experiencing new things — definitely not sitting at home."
— **Heather,** 13, East Stroudsburg, Pennsylvania

In a Word

If you had to describe yourself in one word, what would you say? Are you funny, friendly, creative, or unique? Here's how the girls surveyed summed themselves up. **What's the one word you would use to describe yourself?**

- Fun/outgoing (14%)
- Caring/sweet (12%)
- Friendly/sociable (10%)
- Funny (8%)
- Energetic/hyper (8%)
- Unique (6%)
- Exciting/spontaneous (6%)
- Creative (4%)
- Athletic (4%)
- "Me" (4%)*

Changing Yourself

"I'd like to make my rudeness disappear for life."
— **Kate,** 12, Walnut Creek, California

Let's face it — most people have something about themselves they'd like to change . . . or at least tinker with a little bit! After all, nobody's perfect! The girls we heard from were no different. While some wished they could swap their shyness for a little more self-assurance, others wanted to tame their tendency to show off. The answers we got on this question were proof positive that sometimes what one girl considers a

*Occasionally, throughout this book, the percentages we've listed for a particular section don't add up to 100%. This is because, for some questions, we received many answers that only one or two percent of the girls gave — and to list all these answers would get way too long!

character flaw, another might find an admirable trait.

On the other hand, some girls said they wouldn't change a thing about themselves. Being happy with who you are is a great character trait in and of itself. Even if you do spot some things about yourself you'd like to work on, just remember to give yourself lots of credit for being the great girl that you already are!

Take a look at what some girls might wish for if a magic genie were to appear to grant them their wishes. **In answer to the question "If you could change one thing about yourself, what would it be?" the top five responses were:**

1) Be more outgoing, less shy.
2) Treat people better and not be so rude.
3) Be more patient.
4) Have more self-esteem.
5) Not change a thing!

Happiness Is . . .

No doubt about it, the happiness of a lot of girls is due to the friendships in their lives. Half of the girls we heard from said that hanging out with friends is the thing that makes them happiest. What's a girl to do when her pals aren't around? That's when family comes in — 15% find hanging with their family second in line for making them happiest. And don't forget Fido! Playing with pets came in third as the best way to make them smile.

> **79% of girls feel it's more important to have a great family than a great career.**

But Sadness Is . . .

Since most of the girls surveyed all seem to love their families a lot, it came as no surprise that the thought of losing a family member was at the top of the list of things that would make them sad.

Take a look at the top tearjerkers:

- Losing a family member (41%)
- Having a friend or family member move away (13%)
- Having a pet die (7%)
- Fighting with parents (6%)

25 Things to Do to Brighten Your Mood

When something is making you sad, try beating the blues with these pick-me-up tips:

1) Call your best gal pal and let her cheer you up.

2) Exercise. Studies show that getting your heart rate up can help boost your mood.

3) Rent a funny movie — like *Clueless* or *The Wedding Singer* — and laugh yourself happy.

4) Pamper yourself. Give yourself a manicure or a pedicure to lift your spirits.

5) Write in your journal, or draw or paint a picture. Sometimes just getting your thoughts and emotions down on paper will make you feel better.

6) Help others. Volunteer your services to a friend, parent, or neighbor. Doing something nice for others is a great remedy for the blues and will probably take your mind off your troubles.

7) Play with your pet.

8) Bake something yummy. Then, of course, sample it once it's done!

9) Window-shop at your favorite store.

10) Learn a new hobby. . . . There's no time like the present to take up drawing, dance, or something else you've always had an interest in. Buy a book on the subject or sign up for a class.

11) Turn on some upbeat tunes. Save the sad songs for another time!

12) Soak in the tub with your favorite book and lots of bubbles.

13) Rekindle a friendship. Write a letter or an e-mail to a long-lost friend.

14) Make a friendship bracelet for a bud to remind yourself of how lucky you are to have great pals.

15) Fly a kite, ride your bike, go in-line skating — anything you enjoy and that gets you outside (and outside of yourself). Any kind of physical activity is likely to brighten your outlook.

16) Get advice. If you're upset about a problem you just can't seem to solve, seek advice from a parent, counselor, or trusted adult.

17) Look through your photo albums. Great memories have a way of brightening your outlook on life.

18) Clean your room. Seriously! Cleaning and organizing is good for your mind and your mood.

19) Plan a get-together with friends. Organizing the event will help take your mind off your troubles.

20) Visit the library and explore its shelves. Books can transport you to another place and cheer you up.

21) Try out a new hairstyle. Change your perspective with a look that's altogether different.

22) Take a hike. Grab a pal and go enjoy the outdoors with a little nature walk. When you realize how great the whole wide world is, your problems just may not seem as bad or as big.

23) Start a scrapbook. Dig up old letters, ticket stubs, and other mementos that bring back the good times and organize them in a scrapbook.

24) Check out your horoscope to find brighter days on the horizon.

25) Go to a movie and transport your mind to another place for two hours.

Beauty or Brains?

Fifty-five percent of the girls surveyed would prefer to be smart vs. good-looking. (*"Because if I was smart, I could figure out a way to be beautiful,"* says Lindsey, 14, of Missouri.) The number of votes for brain-power over beauty dropped just a bit when it came to the type of guy they'd like to date: 52% said they'd take the boy with the brains, while 41% want a guy who's good-looking. (And 7% said they couldn't decide — their ideal guy just had to have *both* brains and looks!)

Mirror, Mirror

"I would like to have perfect, flawless skin."
— **Tessa, 14***

Since even supermodels are concerned about their physical flaws, it's pretty clear that absolutely no one thinks they are perfect! But the truth is, when you look in the mirror, the flaws you see are probably not noticed as much by other people.

We asked girls what they would most like to change about their physical appearance. Take a look at the top five responses, then read on for advice on how to improve your self-image.

*When a girl's name, age, or home city and state aren't listed, it's because she didn't include this information on her survey.

The girls we polled said, if they could, they would change this aspect of their appearance:

- Weight   (29%)
- Hair   (18%)
- Skin   (14%)
- Legs   (9%)
- Height   (7%)

Beating the Body Bummers

Don't think your appearance measures up? It's time to take a new look at yourself. It's easy to focus on your flaws when, all around you, you see pictures of models who seem, well, picture-perfect. And then some of your friends might have features that you'd just die to have. Whatever the case, you can take steps to improve your self-image and your self-confidence.

Get over the fact that supermodels look perfect. Supermodel images are enhanced and touched up on all those magazine covers anyway. Look around you — perfect-looking people don't actually exist (although some people, to be sure, are very attractive)! While models have looks that sell magazines and clothes, there's a lot more to being attractive than how you look.

Take a look at the whole you before you come down hard on yourself. Don't focus on your flaws (we all have them) when you're making a judgment about yourself. Instead, focus on your great features (we all have *them*, too!), both on the inside and the outside.

Forget about wishing you had one friend's hair and another's height. For one thing, it's just not going to happen. And furthermore, your friends are probably wishing that they had some of your great features, too.

What about when someone makes a negative comment about your appearance? Turn the other cheek. People who criticize usually have a low opinion of themselves . . . so try not to take it personally.

Talk about it. Finally, if you have such a negative self-image that you are often down, talk to a trusted adult, like a parent or school counselor.

Fright Night!

What are the things that creep girls out the most and show up in nightmares? Creepy crawlers like spiders, snakes, and bugs slithered their way to the top of the list. Also frightening is the thought of losing a family member or friend, followed by the threat of violence.

Where you live also plays a role in what scares you. Just ask 12-year-old Danielle of Homer, Alaska. Her big fear? Bears!

Then of course, *how* you live might also hold some potential horror. Kathleen, 13, of Sterling Heights, Michigan, is most frightened by her room! *"It's a pigsty,"* she claims.

Besides having things that frighten them, some girls have actually experienced truly scary moments. **The top three most terrifying things the surveyed girls have experienced are:**

1) Being lost.
2) Being followed.
3) Hearing strange noises when home alone.

Other frightening moments mentioned included:

"One time my dad, my brother, and me were chased by four big dogs."
— **Elizabeth**, 14, DeMotte, Indiana

"I choked on a cherry at a restaurant."
— **Jacqui**, 13, Plymouth, Wisconsin

"I got lost inside Disney World."
— **Jenny,** 13, Buffalo Grove, Illinois

"I got into a car accident. . . . Luckily, I wasn't hurt."
— **Emily,** 13, Chicago, Illinois

"I was in a tent once and I kept hearing weird noises outside. I never found out what it was. . . . It was either some crazed maniac or a weird creature."
— **Sarah,** 13, New Richmond, Wisconsin

Red-faced Revelations

If you've ever had a mortifying moment — one where you just wanted to crawl under a rock and hide for the rest of your life — you're definitely not alone. Girls everywhere have had moments of complete embarrassment. And while at the time those moments may have seemed horrifying, looking back on them today, they may seem more hilarious than mortifying. Take a look at what makes some girls blush!

What a Trip!

Most of the girls surveyed have probably known how to walk since they were, like, a year old. But that doesn't stop their legs from turning to spaghetti every now and then. No wonder trip-ping, falling, or stumbling top the list of most-common embarrassing moments.

"I was running to my chair in second period when I tripped and fell with the loudest THUD!"
    — **Heather,** 13, East Stroudsburg, Pennsylvania

"I tripped and fell down a flight of stairs at a party."
    — **Lindsey,** 14, Marthasville, Missouri

"I fell off of a stage in music program."
    — **Jenny,** 13, Buffalo Grove, Illinois

"It was my birthday and I was in the sixth grade. After school, I was walking behind my dad with a cupcake in my hand and all of a sudden some older kids yelled, 'Happy Birthday' to me. Well, while I was waving to them my dad stopped [sud-denly] and I hit him with the cupcake. All the older kids laughed."
    — **Christie,** 15, Marion, Arkansas

"I fell in front of my entire class."
    — **Cristen,** 11, Brooklyn, New York

"My friend tripped me and I fell on my butt right in front of my crush."
    — **Sara,** 13, Sierra Vista, Arizona

"I ran into a sign in Kmart and blacked out for two minutes."
— **Samantha,** 13, Garden City, Michigan

All the World's a Stage

Also embarrassing is being singled out in public.

"I had to get on the school's stage and sing 'Happy Birthday' to my friend in front of everyone."
— **Alina,** 13, Missouri City, Texas

"One day I was at the mall. I was in a dressing room at a store trying something on. My mom didn't know where I was so they started calling out my name over the mall's entire PA system."
— **Kathleen,** 13, Sterling Heights, Michigan

I Spy

Ooops! Seeing something you're not supposed to — or being seen by others when you don't think anyone's looking — often is the ultimate embarrassment. Just ask these red-faced girls:

"I was at the beach on a school trip and my bathing suit flew up in front of everyone."
— **Nicole,** 13, Henderson, Nevada

"This woman walked into the bathroom when I was using it at a fast-food restaurant."
— **Deborah,** 14, Brooklyn, New York

"I once walked in a men's rest room when someone was using it."
   — **Emily,** 13, Chicago, Illinois

"My most embarrassing moment was when I sent a letter to the guy I liked. It was only supposed to be to him but the whole school found out."
   — **Morgan,** 11, Bryn Mawr, Pennsylvania

"I was in the bathroom at my house and my brother's friend came running in."
   — **Heather,** 15, Cedar Rapids, Iowa

Body Blahs

Thankfully, we can control our bodily functions . . . most of the time. But on occasion, some girls have lost control — at the absolute worst times!

"When I was in the second grade, I threw up during the Pledge of Allegiance."
   — **Holly,** 11, Suwanee, Georgia

"I was at my friend's house, and I was laughing so hard that I wet my pants."
   — **Anonymous**

"I was riding on the bus and I barfed!"
   — **M.,** 11, Oswego, Illinois

Big Trouble

From what we read, it seems like the girls who filled out our survey are angels most of the time. But we did get a few of them to take off their halos and reveal what the worst thing they've ever done was. The number one answer was lying — to everyone from parents to friends to teachers. **The worst thing they said they've ever done was:**

- Lie to their parents. (17%)
- Lie to a friend. (13%)
- Do or say something really mean
  to a friend. (12%)
- Steal something. (8%)
- Do something without their
  parents' permission. (8%)

"One time, I ordered something on my mom's credit card without her knowledge."
— **Joanna**, 13, Palm Harbor, Florida

"Once when I was getting in trouble, I laughed when the principal was yelling at me."
— **Danielle**, 12, Homer, Alaska

"I told my friend she couldn't come to my sleepover because my mom didn't like her."
— **Mallory**, 12, Merry Hill, North Carolina

"I stole something from a store."
— **Morgan,** 11, Bryn Mawr, Pennsylvania

"I told my friend that a guy she liked wanted to ask her out when he really didn't."
— **Elizabeth,** 14, DeMotte, Indiana

"I told my friend I hated her. I didn't mean it, but she was mad at me and told my mom what I did."
— **Sara,** 13, Sierra Vista, Arizona

Do You Believe?

Where does God fit in your lives? An overwhelming 93% of the girls who completed our survey said that they believe in God. Only 2% said they did not believe in God, while 5% are unsure. Of those who believe in God, 63% said they attend church or synagogue pretty regularly (twice a month or more), while 37% admit they don't attend church or synagogue regularly . . . more like on the major religious holidays only.

Role Models

Mom and Pop came out on top in the role-model category. "Like mother, like daughter" is a compliment for most — nearly 40% of the girls surveyed said they look up to their mom. But a substantial 22% of you view your dad as your biggest role model. Parents rule!

Thirty-five percent of girls look to the big screen or the tube for their role models, with actresses Jennifer Love Hewitt and Drew Barrymore topping the charts. Sarah Michelle Gellar is also admired (perhaps for her vampire-slaying abilities?). **Some other people the girls surveyed look up to are:**

- Friends   (17%)
- Sister(s)   (9%)
- Grandmother   (6%)
- Teacher   (6%)
- Church leader   (4%)

Fast-forward

We asked girls what they imagined the future holds for them and what they thought their life would will be like 15 to 20 years from now. Take a look at their predictions.

Hey, superwomen! Thirty-three percent of the girls surveyed hope they'll be married with both a family and a career in 15 to 20 years, while 25% see themselves on their own but with a career. Twelve percent intend to be married with a family, and 6% think they'll probably be married with a career but no family. Having a nice house 15 to 20 years down the road is also top of the list for

13% of girls. And here's what the rest of the girls hope for in 15 to 20 years:

- To be in school (4%)
- To have a boyfriend, career, and a home (2%)
- To be married (2%)
- Other (3%)

When it comes to careers, more than a few of you have been bitten by the acting bug! Being either an actress, singer, or model is the number one career choice for the majority of the girls surveyed. **Here's a look at the ten most desired jobs for girls like you:**

1) Actress
2) Singer
3) Model
4) Musician
5) Teacher
6) Doctor or Veterinarian
7) Writer
8) Fashion designer
9) Architect
10) Dancer

Sixty-two percent of girls see themselves living in a big city, while 38% prefer the idea of living in a small town.

Chapter Two

Parents, Pals, and Pets

We're happy to report that it's "Home, Sweet Home" for most of the girls who filled out the survey. Well, OK — there are moments when your parents get majorly on your nerves. And oh, boy, can you and your sibs get into big fights! But when things at home get a little rough, we learned that you usually lean on friends for support. In fact, friends are a huge part of your lives. Most of you can think of nothing you'd rather do than just hang out with your pals. But as you'll see as you read on, even the best of buds can have the occasional fight. . . .

All in the Family

Nearly three-quarters of the girls we surveyed (71%) live with both parents, and most have brothers and sisters living at home as well. **Here's a closer look at the typical home life for the girls surveyed:**

- Live with both parents   (71%)
- Live with just Mom   (11%)
- Live with just Dad   (4%)
- Live with their mom and stepfather   (8%)
- Live with their dad and stepmother   (2%)
- Live either with guardians or split their time equally between both Mom and Dad   (4%)

> **According to the 1990 U.S. Census, 27.3% of kids today live in single-parent households. This contrasts with the much smaller percentage (15%) of girls we surveyed who say they live in single-parent homes.**

Judging from the amount of the surveyed girls who have brothers, sisters, or both, home is a pretty noisy place! **Here's the lowdown on the sib situation:**

- Have both brothers and sisters (41%)
- Just have a brother or brothers (28%)
- Just have a sister or sisters (26%)
- Are only children with no siblings (5%)

No family portrait would be complete without including pets! And the girls we surveyed seem to have plenty of 'em! Eighty-nine percent have some sort of critter at home to keep them company. While dogs, cats, and birds are the preferred pets, there were a number of less common animals on the list, too . . . like turtles, and even a hermit crab! **Take a look at which animals made top dog in the pets category:**

- Dogs (65%)
- Cats (43%)
- Birds (13%)
- Hamsters or gerbils (8%)
- Fish (4%)

(This adds up to more than 100% because some girls have more than just one type of pet!)

Home, Sweet Home

We asked girls about their home life, including whether they were happy at home. Ninty-five percent of the girls who live in a household with both parents plus some siblings answered that they were happy with their living situation. Seventy-five percent of the girls who live with their mom and stepdad said that they were happy at home, while just 30% of girls who live with Mom only consider themselves happy at home. And what about dads doing solo duty as parents? Half the girls who live with just Dad give this scenario the thumbs-up. But, as you surely know, no matter how ideal her living situation, every girl has the occasional battle with her parents!

Parent Problems

Face it — you're pretty much stuck with your parents until you turn 18 (and even after that, guess what — they'll still have a major influence on your life). Besides the occasional flare-up within your family, you also have to deal with your parents' quirks and habits (like embarrassing you — whether they mean to or not — in front of your friends).

The good news is that you're not alone in your plight! The surveyed girls spoke up about their parents — the good, the bad, and the totally embarrassing! And they also 'fessed up about some of their not-so-nice behavior as daughters, too.

Parental Offenses

Everything from cheapness to weirdness was mentioned as a parental offense. The Mom and Dad annoyance-meter was at its highest, though, when parents acted overprotective — but many more charges than just that made it to the list! **When we asked girls what their biggest gripe about their parents was, these were the top nine complaints:**

1) They're overprotective.
2) They're closed-minded.
3) They embarrass me.
4) They ignore me.
5) They force me to do chores.
6) They try to run my life.
7) They think they're so cool.
8) They treat me like a little kid.
9) They're unfair.

Here are some highlights from the Parental Hall of Shame:

"My parents are weird . . . but aren't all parents?"
 — **Mahleea,** 11, Lawrence, Kansas

"They make a big deal out of something so small."
— **Nicole**, 13, Carol Stream, Illinois

"They smoke way too much."
— **Alina**, 13, Missouri City, Texas

"They pick my TV stations for me and tell me what I can watch."
— **Shanika**, 10, Hartford, Alabama

"My mom won't let me burp in front of her."
— **Danielle**, 12, Homer, Alaska

"I don't like when they try to sing our music."
— **Lindsey**, 14, Marthasville, Missouri

"My dad is a tightwad!"
— **Pennie**, Burleson, Texas

"They are so annoying in the morning when I have to get up."
— **Morgan**, 11, Bryn Mawr, Pennsylvania

Making Peace with Your Parents: Or, How to Get Along with Them (Nearly) All the Time

Put up the white flag! Call a truce! It's time to put an end to family fights . . . well, to at least give 'em a rest for a while anyway! Believe it or not, getting along with your parents during a time in your life when you pretty much wish they'd stay out of your hair doesn't have to be impossible. But it does require a mix of courtesy, honesty, and knowing when to hold your tongue. Here are some tips to make the task easier:

✴ **Be home on time — but by all means call if you're going to be late.** Many girls fear the wrath of their parents so much that they put off facing their parents until the bitter end. That is, when they know they're going to be late, they don't call home because they dread being punished. Big mistake! The reason most parents are so hard-core about making sure you aren't out late is that one minute past the time when you were supposed to be home they start worrying that something awful has happened to you. And the later you are, the more they worry, so that by the time you finally do stroll in, they're so worried and upset that they enter into major yell mode. Not only that, but once you've put them through that misery, they're less likely to trust you in the future. Bottom line: Do your best to make it home in time, but if you can't, make a phone call.

✴ **Try the truth.** A lot of girls waste time

and energy coming up with elaborate lies that their parents see right through. Even for smooth liars, there are big problems that arise from fibbing. First, lies have a way of catching up with you. You know — you forget exactly what it was you told your parents, or you forget to fill all your friends in on what your story is and they end up blowing it. Second, since your parents were once your age, they most likely know firsthand about fibbing to parents. You may not give them credit for it, but they do have a clue! And third, getting caught in a lie has much worse consequences than just telling the truth in the first place. Telling the truth will earn your parents' trust, which will make your life so much easier!

✳ **Fight fire with reason.** When you sense you're getting a rotten deal, avoid the usual whining, yelling, or pouting and instead present your case logically and rationally. Like, if your mom has said, "No way!" to an outfit you really just have to have, instead of begging, pleading, or buying it and wearing it behind her back, talk to her about her reasons for not letting you buy it. Once you know what her objections are, then you can focus on how to overcome them. If it's a money issue, try and come up with the cash yourself.

If Mom thinks the outfit is too old for you, ask her for acceptable alternatives that would work. You might be surprised — talking things out with your parents can have some pretty good consequences.

✳ **Choose your battles.** There are probably certain things that you do that always rile your parents and that aren't a big deal for you to stop doing. For example, if you know your parents' biggest concern is for you to get good grades, make sure your homework is done before you ask them if you can go out with your friends. Because if you haven't finished your homework, you *know* they're not gonna let you go — then a fight may ensue. When there are things you know you won't get past your parents, don't even bother with those battles.

✳ **Accept that life can be unfair.** There are going to be times when things really stink — like when your parents make what seem to be unreasonable rules or when they forbid you to do what you want to do. If you are unable to convince them otherwise, even though it's tough, get over it and move on. How you handle this situation could also make getting your way easier the next time.

Liar, Liar

When the going gets tough, the tongue starts wagging! A whopping 87% of the girls surveyed admitted that they've lied to their parents. (And who knows if the other 13% were actually telling the truth!) The fibs ranged from topics such as boys to not doing chores to bugging your little brother. Many girls have lied to their parents too many times to count! What's all the fibbing about? **Here's the list of topics the girls were most likely to lie about:**

- Where they're going/where
  they've been   (21%)
- Spending time with boys   (11%)
- Not doing chores   (9%)
- Coming home late   (8%)
- Whether homework is done   (6%)
- Your friends   (4%)
- Fighting with siblings   (4%)
- Skipping school   (4%)
- Grades   (4%)

"I lied to my parents about how my hamster died. . . . It really died because I didn't feed it."
   — **Kate,** 12, Walnut Creek, California

"I didn't tell my parents that I have Marilyn Manson CDs."
— **Lindsey,** 14, Marthasville, Missouri

"I told my parents I didn't have candy in my room when I really did."
— **Haley,** 10, Leechburg, Pennsylvania

"They don't know that I had a boyfriend."
— **Jenny,** 13, Buffalo Grove, Illinois

"There are too many to just pick one!"
— **Emily,** 13, Chicago, Illinois

"I lied about why I was out past my curfew."
— **Nicole,** 13, Henderson, Nevada

Now You're Really in Trouble

No surprise here — getting caught in a lie has gotten most of the girls surveyed into big-time trouble with their parents. Coming home late is also grounds for parental punishment, followed by talking back to parents and fighting with brothers and sisters. The usual sentence or punishment? Getting grounded.

"The worst trouble I got in was being caught lying. I got grounded for three months."
    — **Brandy,** 15

"Once, I forged my parents' signature on a school paper (a math test). They found out and they weren't too happy."
    — **Lindsey,** 15, Pennsylvania

"I got put on restriction for talking back to my parents."
    — **Nancy,** 14, Macon, Georgia

"I got grounded for a weekend for beating up on my brothers."
    — **Emily,** 15, Ohio

"I got a huge long-distance telephone bill for almost a thousand dollars!"
    — **Tessa,** 14

Disaster Zones and Other Parental Hazards

More than half the girls surveyed told us that having a messy room gets them in loads of trouble. But that's not all! **The things parents give them a hard time about were:**

- Having a messy room (59%)
- Not doing their chores (57%)
- Not spending enough time on schoolwork (56%)
- Talking on the telephone too much (50%)
- Their choice of friends (43%)
- The clothes they wear (35%)
- Wearing makeup (22%)
- Their hairstyle (13%)
- Other: Fighting with brothers and/or sisters, their grades, not listening to or interrupting their folks (19%)

Sister Squabbles

With so many sisters in the picture, it's pretty much a guarantee that there will be a little feuding from time to time. **Just what are the sister troubles all about? Take a peek:**

- Anything and everything! (13%)
- Taking each other's stuff (11%)
- Clothes (9%)
- Having to share a room (4%)
- Snooping in each other's stuff (3%)

Even with the occasional battle, there's still something special about having a sister. Katherine, 12, of Duncan, Oklahoma, sums it up this way:

"I think sisters are great because they are always there to talk or to play with (even though my sister does want to play sometimes while I am busy). We do get into some arguments, but they usually just disappear after a while. Our family loves to travel in the car, and when we do, my sister and I can always come up with fun things to do to make the ride better. Even though she gets annoying and can sometimes be rude, she will always be my sister and my best friend."

Tattletale Troubles

When it comes to keeping quiet about their brothers' and sisters' troubles, only one-third of the girls we heard from say that they've never snitched on a sibling. The other two-thirds have occasionally spilled the beans on sibling secrets. It seems like most girls will run blabbing to Mom and Dad if it means getting a brother or sister in trouble. But there are good reasons for involving parents in your sib's business — like if a brother or sister is doing something that could really get them in trouble, for example stealing or cutting school.

"I tell my parents just about anything to get my sister in trouble."
— **Christi**, 15, Franklin, Kentucky

"I told my parents about my brother getting his nipple pierced. I thought it was gross!"
— **Christie**, 15, Marion, Arkansas

"When I was little, I used to tell my mom all of the dirt I scooped up about my sister. She deserved it — she was so mean to me."
— **Leona**, Palmyra, New Jersey

In Friends We Trust

To be a true friend you've got to be trustworthy — that's what the girls surveyed made perfectly clear. No best-friend feature was more important to you than trust. Even the number two response — honesty — reinforces the first and makes it clear that being able to rely on your pals to be loyal and tight-lipped means a lot more than anything else. **The top ten most important qualities in a friend are:**

1) Trustworthiness
2) Honesty
3) Friendliness

4) Sense of humor
5) Caring
6) Fun
7) Loyalty
8) Positive attitude
9) Understanding
10) Reliability (being there for you)

"Melissa is my best friend. We have been BF's since kindergarten. She's always energetic, fun, there to talk to, understanding, helpful, full of great advice. To describe her in a word, I would say 'majestic.'"
— **Maria,** San Jose, California

"My best friend is Teylor. We've been best friends for nine years. She's fun and energetic. One word to describe her is 'outgoing.'"
— **Heather,** 15, Cedar Rapids, Iowa

"My best friend and I have been friends for only two years, but it feels like forever. She's crazy!"
— **Deborah,** 14, Brooklyn, New York

"My best friend is my German shepherd, Jack. In one word — he's jumpy!"
— **Mahleea,** 11, Lawrence, Kansas

"Jill has been my best friend since the third grade. She and I have never fought and I think that she is fun and would call her awesome."
— **Anonymous,** 13

"I have three best friends. We have been friends for almost a year and are very close. We all understand each other and respect each other, too."
— **Amanda,** 13, Pensacola, Florida

Fun with Friends

What do girls and their friends like to do for fun? Sounds like just being with buds is all it takes to have a blast. Just hanging out together was by far the top choice for what girls wanna do with their friends. One thing's for sure — girls know how to have fun! **Here's a look at the top fifteen favorite friend festivities:**

1) Hanging out
2) Going to the movies
3) Shopping
4) Talking
5) Going to the mall
6) Going to the pool/swimming
7) Playing sports
8) Going to parties

9) In-line skating
10) Riding bikes
11) Going to the park
12) Dancing
13) Listening to music
14) Going bowling
15) Having sleepovers

Boredom Busters: Ten Great Ideas for Having Fun with Friends

Don't let dullness put a damper on your friendships! Be creative when coming up with things to do with your friends. Here are ten ideas to help get you started:

1) *Do the mall crawl:* Head to the nearest shopping center for a little people-watching and clothes shopping. No dough? No problem. Try on the most outrageous outfits you can find (you know you'd never buy them anyway!) just for fun.

2) *Get on-line:* There's a ton to do in cyber-space just a few clicks of the mouse away. On a rainy day you and a bud can visit Web sites designed just for girls, play on-line games, check out current

events, listen to music, shop — and lots of other stuff!

3) Bake a treat: Whip up a batch of cookies or some cool fruit smoothies with your pals, then enjoy your concoction.

4) Play a game: Dig through the board games stashed in the closet (Monopoly, anyone?) or come up with your own games, like charades or truth or dare. Or if the weather is nice, grab a group of girls and go miniature golfing or play a game of doubles tennis.

5) Spin some tunes: You and your friends can combine your music collections and listen to your hearts' content. Come up with different 10 All-Time Greatest Songs lists — like the 10 best songs about cars, the 10 best songs sung by teenagers, 10 best sound tracks, etc. Or if you wanna hear some new music, head to the music store and check out the listening stations to hear dozens of different CDs.

6) Try new 'dos: Put your beauty talents to work by giving each other totally different hairdos.

7) **Be stars:** Call your local radio station and make goofy song requests, then listen for them to be played.

8) **Get sporty:** Get a friend or two together and take a hike, ride a bike, go for a blade, or make a splash. . . . There are tons of athletic activities to keep you busy no matter the weather or the time of year.

9) **Catch a flick:** So what if you and your buds have already seen all the biggies. Expand your horizons by taking in a foreign film or an old classic.

10) **Be silly:** Throw reason out the door and leave nothing off-limits! Come up with a new, crazy dance step together, write love letters to your crushes (then make sure they never see them!), or put together the tackiest outfits you can and then wear them out to a fast-food joint — and see how long you can keep serious, straight faces!

Keeping in Touch

We asked the girls we polled how they reach out and touch their friends and how much time they spend keeping in touch. Do they phone, e-mail, or meet up in person? **Here's the lowdown on how much time is spent with friends.**

Call Me!: Most girls spend between one and three hours a week talking on the telephone with pals.

Cyber buds: While nearly half the girls report that they don't use e-mail, the rest of 'em set aside an hour a week to e-mail friends.

Get-togethers: Being there with buds is definitely the best way to go! Most girls say they spend ten or more hours per week just hanging out with friends.

"My best friend and I have been friends since the second grade, and now we are going into high school. She's the greatest because she's got a great personality. . . . She's the greatest friend ever."
— **Heather,** 13, East Stroudsburg, Pennsylvannia

"My best friend is myself because I can keep secrets and don't pressure myself into doing things."
— **Jacqui,** 13, Plymouth, Wisconsin

"My best friend Lauren and I have been friends for almost two years. She's an awesome dancer and gymnast."
— **Mallory,** 12, Merry Hill, North Carolina

Dishing It Out

How well do girls keep secrets? And how well do their friends keep their lips zipped shut when asked to? The verdict on keeping quiet is in — take a look at the results: When it comes to having loose lips with friends' secrets, it's nearly half and half. Fifty-one percent of girls said that, yes, they have revealed a secret that a friend entrusted to them, while 49% said they have never given away a friend's secret.

"I told my friend's boyfriend that she cheated on him. We got in a huge fight, but now we're best friends again."
— **Alina,** 13, Missouri City, Texas

"I've never told a friend's secret. I think keeping secrets is part of being a good friend."
— **Mahleea,** 11, Lawrence, Kansas

"I knew my friend liked this guy, but she told me not to tell him. But I thought he liked her so I

told him. Well, he did like her and they started dating."
— **Christie**, 14, Marion, Arkansas

"I've never spilled the beans!"
— **M.**, 11, Oswego, Illinois

So while half the girls surveyed say they are totally trustworthy, it seems like they can't say the same for their friends! Two-thirds have had a friend or best friend reveal something about them that they swore to secrecy! Most of the time friends had the hardest time keeping quiet about crushes. (And isn't there a part of you that really wants him to know anyway?!)

"My friend told a guy that I liked him, but we ended up going out so it was OK."
— **Samantha**, 13, Garden City, Michigan

"My friend told everyone who it was I liked. . . . We aren't friends anymore."
— **Tessa**, 14

"My friend went right up to my crush and told him I liked him, when I was standing right there with them!"
— **Nancy,** 14, Macon, Georgia

Revealing friends' secrets to other kids your age is one thing, but snitching — confessing friends' less-than-perfect behavior to an adult — is something most girls just won't do, unless they sense a friend is getting herself into big trouble. Only 29% said that they've snitched on a friend. The top reason for tattling was when they found out a friend was smoking, and felt they needed to tell an adult to get her to stop. Still, though, most girls would rather help a friend deal with a problem themselves rather than blabbing to a grown-up, as 79% were loud and clear about not snitching on buds — ever.

"My friend once lied to a teacher. I told the teacher she was lying but she didn't wind up getting in trouble."
— **Morgan,** 11, Bryn Mawr, Pennsylvania

"I once told the principal that a girl lived in another city because her mom was lying about where she lived so she could go to our school."
— **Kate,** 12, Walnut Creek, California

"Have I ever snitched on a friend? No way! Are you crazy?"
— **Megan,** 13, Newport Beach, California

Friend Stories

"Natalie is my best friend. It's hard to describe her so briefly because she's perfect in every way. We never fight and she always listens and feels free to express her feelings. Even though she's been home-schooled for three years, we're still best friends."
— **Emily,** 14, Westerville, Ohio

"My best friend Jeremy and I have been friends for four years. He's very protective of me and sweet."
— **Lindsey,** 14, Marthasville, Missouri

Chapter Three
Book Talk

School is definitely the place where the girls who answered our survey spend the most time, so it's not surprising that they had a lot to say about what's going on in those halls! And nope — it's not just about reading, writing, and arithmetic. There's plenty more to fill the days during the school year. There are some troubling things going on in schools today, and girls were up-front about the things that bum them out the most. They were also pretty up-front about troubles with teachers.

Class Acts

Which are the classes that girls like you get the most out of? And which do they wish they could make disappear? **Take a look — the classes or subjects girls love (OK, maybe just like a lot) are:**

- English (19%)
- Gym/P.E. (15%)
- Language arts (13%)
- Science (13%)
- Math (11%)
- Art (11%)

Two percent of girls said that they were home-schooled, making it a little tough to pick out a fave class.

Not all classes are that thrilling, though. There are some that the girls surveyed just wished would go away to put them out of their misery! Number-crunchers they're not — the least favorite class (by far) was math. **The classes or subjects the girls we surveyed liked least are:**

- Math (33%)
- Social studies (17%)
- Science (13%)
- History (7%)
- Gym/P.E. (7%)
- English (7%)

Trouble at School

For the girls who answered our survey, peer pressure, something that's been around forever (even back in your parents' school days), still plagues most schools and ranks as the number one school problem. Coming in a surprising second on the list is smoking — girls were pretty clear about the fact that they do *not* think lighting up is cool. And if there's any doubt that girls today are serious about their studies, just check out number three on the list of what they consider bad about school: poor grades and low scholastic achievement. **Here's the lowdown on what's lame at school:**

- Peer pressure   (52%)
- Smoking   (48%)
- Grades/poor scholastic
  achievement   (43%)
- Kids with too many family
  problems   (31%)
- Lack of moral values   (30%)

Campus Crimes

Our correspondents took off their halos to reveal a few things about their school behavior. Sometimes, it seems, the temptation to take a look at a friend's answers on a test, or to just blow off school for a day, is too strong to resist.

Your Cheatin' Hearts

The confessions are in: 62% of girls said they've cheated on a test.

"I cheated on a test in Spanish class — I forgot how to spell summer *in Spanish."*
— **Sara,** 13, Sierra Vista, Arizona
(Note to Sara: It's *verano!*)

"I cheated once when I sat next to a brainiac."
— **Emily,** 15, Ohio

"I looked at someone else's answers (only to the hard questions)."
— **Nancy,** 14, Macon, Georgia

But even more of the girls surveyed said they'd cheated on an assignment than on a test. Two-thirds admitted to getting a little "help" from their friends on homework . . . and a few even relied on Mom to do the job!

"I once brought home an assignment for my mom to do."
— **Natalie,** 15, Charenton, California

"I forgot to do my homework, so my friend next to me on the bus gave the answers to me, then I gave them to a friend, then he gave them to a friend."
— **Amanda**, 13, Pensacola, Florida

"I've never cheated. I think that in order to do well in a class you have to do the homework yourself."
— **Lindsey**, 15, Pennsylvania

The Dish on Ditching

Every now and then, dragging yourself out of bed and getting to school can be a real bummer. Maybe that's why 34% of the girls we asked said that they've skipped school before. Not a huge shocker, but what was surprising was who their partner in crime often was when they skipped — their moms! When it comes to ditching for a day, seems like Mom is the perfect accomplice! **Here's what the girls said when we asked if they'd ever skipped school:**

"Yes . . . I was too tired to think so I hung out with friends."
— **Deborah**, 14, Brooklyn, New York

"Yes — my mom took me to a fair."
— **Anonymous**, 13

51

"I went snowboarding (my mom took me)."
— **Kate,** 12, Walnut Creek, California

"Two days in a row, my mom took me to the mall."
— **Megan,** 13, Newport Beach, California

Going Postal

Passing notes is so normal that nearly every girl confessed that she's been known to send notes to a pal or two during class. (At least it's brushing up on those writing skills, right?) Eighty-five percent of girls sent notes via the desk express. And while 57% are supersly when it comes to passing notes on the fly, 43% have had their notes snatched by a teacher, and some have even (gulp!) had them read in front of the class!

Do the Crime, Pay the Time

Thirteen percent of the girls surveyed can put their halos right back on — they claimed they've never been in any kind of trouble at school. As for the other 87% . . . well, you can't always be perfect, right? The most common form of punishment for bad school behavior was definitely detention, followed by paying a visit to the principal's office. **Here's a peek at the top five bad behaviors that got girls in trouble:**

1) Talking out of turn
2) Fighting
3) Passing notes
4) Not doing homework
5) Breaking the school dress code

That's My Story, and I'm Sticking to It!

No doubt about it — sometimes school can be a real pressure cooker. And sometimes, you girls just run out of time to get all your work done. Unfortunately, most teachers won't accept the "I just didn't have enough time!" excuse. That's why nearly half of those surveyed have had to resort to coming up with a good, fake reason as to why they couldn't turn in that assignment. Most girls try to blame a pesky brother or sister for not being able to turn in their projects, while others came up with some real doozies! **Take a look at some favorites (but don't get any ideas!):**

"I told the teacher my brother scribbled on it."
— **Kate,** 12, Walnut Creek, California

"My dog really did eat my homework once!"
— **Anonymous,** 13

"I said I left it at my dad's house in California. . . . He doesn't even live there."
— **Kelly,** 13, Gold Hill, Oregon

"I said my bro got mad and ripped it up."
— **Samantha,** 13, Garden City, Michigan

"I told my teacher my mom threw it out."
— **Nicole,** 13, Carol Stream, Illinois

"I said I left it in a friend's car."
— **Mallory,** 12, Merry Hill, North Carolina

"I told her that my backpack got stolen and all my stuff was in it."
— **Cindy,** 15, Redwood City, California

Dress Code

Half of the girls we heard from said that they are either required to wear a uniform or to follow a dress code. **Here's a list of a few of the fashions schools are saying is just not acceptable:**

- Short shorts or skirts
- Spaghetti straps
- Tank tops
- T-shirts
- Shirts that are untucked
- Baggy pants
- Low-cut clothes

The jury is still out on uniforms. More and more schools are starting to require them. We heard from girls who believed that uniforms put everyone on an equal playing ground — there's no more passing judgment about people by what they're wearing. Most girls, however, still aren't convinced about the merits of a uniform, feeling that uniforms take away individuality, the right to express oneself, and the freedom of choice. **We asked, "Do you think uniforms are a good idea?"**

- 48% said no
- 31% said yes
- 21% were unsure

Here's why girls are saying yes or no to uniforms:

"Yes, because then you won't be judged on your clothing style."
— **Anonymous**, 13

"No, because everyone looks the same and it's scary."
— **Nicole**, 13, Carol Stream, Illinois

"Yes, that way no one can make fun of what you are wearing."
— **Samantha**, 13, Garden City, Michigan

"No, because we should be free to wear what we want."
— **Haley**, 10, Leechburg, Pennsylvania

"Heck no! Would you want to wear the same thing every day?"
— **Kathleen**, 13, Sterling Heights, Michigan

"Yes, 'cause you can still show your personality through your hairdos and shoes."
— **Heather**, 13, East Stroudsburg, Pennsylvania

"No, because people can't be individuals."
— **Charissa**, 14, Meomonee Falls, Wisconsin

"Yes, because if someone can't afford name brand clothes, they get teased. [This way] we could all be alike."
— **Jacqui**, 13, Plymouth, Wisconsin

Chapter Four

Let the Fun Begin

When school's out (and even when it's in!), it's playtime. No big shocker here — girls definitely like to have fun! Opportunities for having a great time are endless. Shopping may still be majorly popular, but no way are sports any longer just for boys. Girls are joining teams left and right, and discovering more and more that physical activity is an awesome way to hang out with friends and have fun. Quiet time is also important, so doing things like reading books, surfing the Net, and hanging out in their rooms also come up high on girls' list of extracurricular or after-school activities. **Here's a look at what the girls we heard from like to do in their spare time:**

- Hang out with friends   (98%)
- Listen to music   (94%)

- Read magazines (93%)
- Shop (87%)
- Talk on the telephone (83%)
- Watch TV (80%)
- Go to the mall (78%)
- Play sports (67%)
- Write letters or e-mails (63%)
- Read books (52%)
- Play videos/CD-ROMs (31%)
- Participate in school clubs (20%)

The Hobby Lobby

Look out, guys! From the sound of it, girls are taking over the sports world. Playing sports is the number one hobby among girls. Take a look at other favorite hobbies. Maybe you'll get inspired to take one up! **The top ten hobbies are:**

1) Playing sports
2) Shopping
3) Collecting things
4) Listening to music
5) Dancing
6) Reading/Writing
7) Playing a musical instrument
8) Hanging out with friends/talking to friends on the phone
9) Crafts
10) Drawing

Get Sporty!

There's no sitting on the sidelines for this generation! A whopping 80% of the girls we heard from play sports ranging from basketball and soccer to hockey and martial arts. **The top five sports to play are:**

1) Soccer and basketball (tie)
2) Softball and volleyball (tie)
3) Cheerleading
4) Track, swimming, and tennis (three-way tie)
5) Football

No Barriers

Don't think you can cut it when it comes to sports? Well, think again. Soccer star Mia Hamm is a perfect example of someone who didn't let her age or being female get in the way of achieving her goal of becoming a world-class soccer player. This superstar athlete won accolades for being the youngest player ever to play with the U.S. National Team at age 15. When she helped the U.S. team take home the world victory in 1991, she was the youngest player on a team ever to do so. Eight years later, in 1999, Mia Hamm and the rest of the women on the U.S. team won yet another World Cup.

What makes this five-time recipient of the U.S. Soccer Athlete of the Year award even cooler is her dedication to a very good cause. Following her brother's death in 1996 from aplastic anemia, Mia pledged to make a difference by helping others who suffer from the illness. So she formed the Mia Hamm Foundation to help those battling bone marrow diseases. "My goal is to leave a positive and lasting legacy in the research of bone marrow diseases and for every female athlete to have the opportunity to play the sports they love," says Hamm, an unstoppable athlete and a super role model!

Spectator Stats

Eighty-nine percent of the girls surveyed said that they also like to watch sports. **Here's a look at what you're tuning into on TV or going to see live in stadiums:**

1) Basketball
2) Football
3) Gymnastics and baseball (tie)

4) Soccer
5) Cheerleading competitions and hockey (tie)

Going Surfing

More and more girls are making their way to the Internet, and though e-mail has definitely not replaced talking on the telephone, you're finding that electronic mail is a great way to communicate with both local and out-of-town friends. Sixty-five percent of the girls surveyed have e-mail accounts or access to an e-mail address. And for those with access to the Web, surfing sites is something you're spending plenty of time on. **We asked girls how much time they spend surfing the Internet and this is the result:**

- One or more hours per day   (26%)
- Four to five hours per week   (6%)
- Two hours per week   (9%)
- One hour per week   (3%)
- Less than an hour per week   (19%)
- One to two hours per month   (7%)
- None—they don't have access to the Internet   (30%)

Site-Seeing: Cool Web Sites for Girls

If you're new to the Net, or even if you're a seasoned surfer, you'll want to check out these very cool sites:

- Yahooligans: *www.yahooligans.com* — Start your surfing and your searching here. This site will help you find just about anything on the Internet.
- Brain Teasers: *www.eduplace.com/math/brain* — This site has fun games to play and puzzles to master. You can even win prizes!
- Celebrity Sightings: *www.celebritysightings.com* — Check out this site to find out the latest info on the hottest stars, chat with other girls about celebs, see great star pics, play cool games, and much more.
- Planet Girl: *www.planetgirl.com* — This site has cool short stories and poems written by girls, plus quizzes, chats, bulletin boards, and book and music reviews.
- IndyGirl: *www.indygirl.com* — If you like sports (especially extreme ones), this site is for you! Meet other girls with a passion for sports, and read sports stories and tips just for girls.

- A Girl's World: *www.agirlsworld.com* — A site that's totally powered by girls. Check it out to meet a virtual pen pal, enter contests, chat with other girls, get advice, and read about famous women.

Girls Love a Mystery

Girls' bookshelves are loaded with everything from adventure stories to classics, but it's pretty clear that it's suspense that keeps 'em turning those pages. **The surveyed girls' favorite types of books to read are:**

- Thrillers/mystery/suspense books   (85%)
- Books about celebrities   (59%)
- Fashion and beauty books   (52%)
- Romantic fiction   (44%)
- Adventure books   (39%)
- Books about animals   (28%)
- Books about athletes   (24%)
- Science fiction books   (15%)
- Inspirational/uplifting stories   (13%)
- Historical fiction   (11%)
- Biographies of famous people   (9%)

What a Trip!

Ah, the family vacation — trekking across the country with the 'rents, the sibs, and even pets if you've got 'em! Family vacations provide tons of memories . . . some favorable and some you'd rather forget.

When it comes to fave vacations, you can thank Mickey, Minnie, and the gang for some great times. More girls mentioned Disneyland and Walt Disney World getaways than any other vacation destination as their greatest time ever.

"My favorite vacation was a road trip with my dad to New York City."
— **Anonymous**, Falmouth, Maine

"I went to Europe. I can't describe it. . . . It was so cool and beautiful that I don't know what to say!"
— **Megan**, 13, Newport Beach, California

"My favorite vacation was to Virginia. I went shopping, hung out with my brother, rode roller coasters, and went to the beach."
— **Sara**, 13, Sierra Vista, Arizona

"Disney World!"
— **Holly**, 11, Suwanee, Georgia

"Spokane, Washington . . . I met a cute guy."
— **Jenny,** 13, Buffalo Grove, Illinois

"My best trip was to Florida. We went to Disney World and a water park and made new friends."
— **Jessica,** 12, St. Clair Shores, Michigan

Of course, not all vacations are as wonderful as the ones mentioned above. Almost everyone has had a vacation that left her longing for home! Whether it's due to bad weather, being the only person around who's young, or getting a little *too* close to nature, some girls told us about experiences that make staying home sound pretty good!

"I went up north and was the only one my age there. I had nothing to do!"
— **Jacqui,** 13, Plymouth, Wisconsin

"We went to Yosemite and I got 27 bee stings."
— **Kate,** 12, Walnut Creek, California

"We went to Florida and it rained the whole time."
— **Cristen,** 11, Brooklyn, New York

"A week with my petty cousins who kept making fun of me."
— **Emily,** 14, Westerville, Ohio

"I went to Dallas. It was very hot and I stayed in a nasty hotel."
— **Alina,** 13, Missouri City, Texas

Survival 101: How to Handle the Disaster Vacation

Nothing is worse than being hundreds of miles from home, bored, miserable, and with no way out! But no matter the circumstances, there *are* ways to make even the most awful vacation a little more pleasant. Here are some hints:

❈ **Pack a pal.** Having a friend around can make even the lamest place on earth seem more fun. So the next time you're going on a trip, ask your parents if you can bring along a bud.

❈ **Bring along tons of books and magazines.** Not every moment of your vacation is going to be action-packed. There will no doubt be time spent in a car, plane, train, or bus. You're less likely to be bored or edgy if you are entertained, so pack as many good books and magazines as you can find. Having a stash of reading material is also helpful in case you travel to somewhere where bad weather keeps you indoors.

✳ **Take pictures.** So you're stuck in the middle of nowhere and there's not a thing to do? Get out the camera and start snapping pictures. Come up with the funniest examples of this bad vacation you can find. If you're stuck there, might as well laugh about it later! Maybe it's the tumbleweeds you're surrounded by or a dismal hotel in the middle of nowhere. Snap a shot of it! Then when you get home, you can relive and laugh about the trip with your friends.

✳ **Write it down.** Share your horror stories with the girls back home. Send them postcards and letters describing your vacation. Or bring a travel journal or diary with you to record your personal thoughts.

✳ *Play road games.* If reading in the car makes your stomach churn, a good alternative is to play road games to help pass the time. Create a car bingo game. Make boards with 25 boxes (five rows, five columns) and write in each box things you're likely to see on the road like a deer, an out-of-state license plate, McDonald's, a police officer on a motorcycle, a red sports car, a street sign that says *Main Street*, a radio station billboard — you name it! Be sure the items are arranged differently on each card, then distribute them to all players. Mark off boxes as you see them. The first one to mark off a whole row of items yells, "Car Bingo!" and wins the game.

Chapter Five

The Style Files

The way girls dress and decorate their rooms is a form of personal expression — it's a way to put a style stamp on their surroundings. That's why it would be really unlikely to find someone who dressed just like you or had a room that looked exactly like yours — because everyone's different.

The girls surveyed shared what it was that made their rooms cool and unique, and how their clothes fit into their lifestyle. Read on for the scoop on style, and learn how to add a touch of your own personality to your personal space.

Gimme Shelter

Each girl we heard from told us that her room is truly her sanctuary. It's where she spends a ton of time just hanging out and doing the things she loves. Even if they have to share a room with a brother or sister, the girls we surveyed say they still find ways to make their space unique and special.

We got the lowdown on how girls manage to make their rooms totally "them," from the colors of their walls to what's covering 'em (hint — lots of pictures and posters of cute celebs). Of course, while we can't describe the room of every girl surveyed, there were some decorating schemes that the girls shared in common.

Color Me Blue

Blue is the hue that covers most girls' walls, followed by white, lavender, and pink. And pics of the Backstreet Boys and 'N Sync are also on quite a few walls! Posters of other music, movie, and TV celeb hotties are posted up as well. Female stars are represented, too, as pics of celebs like Drew Barrymore or Jennifer Love Hewitt are also plastered up. A few of you even said that your walls were so covered with posters that you didn't even know what color they were!

Having furry friends of the stuffed variety scattered around is another room feature many girls mentioned. Beanie Babies seemed to be the most popular stuffed critters.

Postcards from friends, pictures of girls and their buds, movie stubs, and other mementos also help make girls' rooms truly unique and a warm, welcoming place to hang out. **Here are some more decoration details:**

"My room is pink . . . and on the walls there are a lot of posters of Ryan Phillipe, Freddie Prinze Jr., Drew Barrymore, and Jennifer Love Hewitt."
— **Heather,** 13, East Stroudsburg, Pennsylvania

"My room has sky-blue paint with yellow-and-white wallpaper with flowers. I have cool posters and pictures of friends everywhere! I have a lava lamp and a bunch of big stuffed animals."
— **Christie,** 15, Marion, Arkansas

"The color of my room is blue and pink. I have cat stuff everywhere. There are posters of cats and of Buffy the Vampire Slayer."
— **Jessica,** 12, San Marcos, Texas

"My room is blue. . . . I have a blue blow-up chair, a futon, glow-in-the-dark stars on my ceiling as they really are up in the sky, pictures of my family on my walls, dried flowers, pompoms from school events, spritzers on my dresser, dream catchers,

71

crystals, my belt from Tae Kwon Do, my cat asleep on my bed, and a chain of stuffed animals hanging from the ceiling."

— **Maria,** San Jose, California

"My walls are covered with Backstreet Boys posters!"

— **Deborah,** 14, Brooklyn, New York

"My room is pastel pink, green, and blue, with a cute flowered bedspread and matching window-seat cover. I have paintings on my walls and ten pastel-colored teacups on a shelf. I have a white TV, phone, and furniture. I also have two large stuffed animals (tiger and bear) — almost as big as me — next to my bed."

— **Emily,** 15, Ohio

"My room is whitish-yellow, with lots and lots of posters and lots of Ty Beanie Babies all over the floor."

— **Sara,** 13, Sierra Vista, Arizona

"My room is awesome. It's painted blue — alien posters everywhere, my doors decorated with pogs and pictures, tons of pictures everywhere, a glow-in-the-dark blow-up chair. You just have to see it! It's my favorite place."

— **Leona,** Palmyra, New Jersey

Personalizing Your Space

Does your room need a little sprucing up? It doesn't take major bucks or a big room to place your stamp of style on your surroundings — creating a personal haven just requires a little creativity. No matter what your budget or your living situation, try out some of these ideas to add a little personal pizzazz to your place.

✳ **Deck the walls.** Painting your room is relatively inexpensive (especially if you and your folks do it yourselves), and a new paint job can make a huge change in your room's overall appearance. If you can't decide on the perfect color, why not choose a shade that reveals your personality? Here are some common colors and what they say about you:

- *Blue*: Peace and harmony. This shade is said to help calm and relax. If you like blue, you're likely thoughtful, caring, and pretty mellow.
- *Pink*: Playful and young. This color is sweet and feminine. If you like pink, you're probably sweet and loving, with an active imagination and a creative flair.

- *Yellow*: Radiant and upbeat. Sunshine yellow represents fun and laughter. Love yellow? You're likely perky and playful.
- *White*: Peaceful, pure, and clean. White can bring a sense of order to a place. If white's your color choice, you're probably orderly and detail-oriented.
- *Purple*: Glamorous and exciting. It's a color that can stir up emotions. If you are a purple person, then you're probably passionate, creative, and a little intense.
- *Green*: Peaceful and harmonious. Nature's favorite color can have a calming effect and promote balance and harmony. Girls who go for green tend to be easygoing and deal with problems in a calm, rational way.

Painting isn't the only way to give new life to your walls — you can also try out fun, colorful wallpaper or wallpaper borders.

✻ **Make a memory board.** If you have scattered pictures and mementos lying around your room, you can turn them into an awesome, inexpensive wall covering. Buy corkboard and colorful stickpins and frame the edges of the board with decorative ribbon glued on. Then arrange pictures, postcards, movie stubs — you name it! — on the board and secure with pins. You can even give your board a title. Hang the board on your wall at eye level for instant great memories.

❋ **Don't hide your hobbies.** What you love to do says a lot about you, so why not proudly display your interests? Like, if you love to collect stuffed animals, put a shelf up high in your room and arrange your furry friends for all to see. Or if soccer's your passion, why not show prints of your fave soccer stars, framed pictures of you and the team, and any awards you've received.

❋ **Make up your bed.** If you've been stuck with the same bedspread since childhood, consider an update. You can, of course, buy new bedding, or if you're handy with a sewing machine, you can make a new cover for an old comforter by sewing together two flat sheets — a more economical option than buying a whole new comforter. Or cover up your old comforter with a cool blanket and buy throw pillows to match your new look. You might even want to add matching curtains.

✳ Fix up your furniture. Maybe your dresser needs a new coat of paint or your desk could do with a few new desktop accessories. There are plenty of ways to update and personalize your furniture without going out and buying a new set. Try adding colorful knobs to a dull dresser for an instant pick-me-up, or if your room is lacking furniture, add an inexpensive inflatable chair in a shade that matches your room.

Clothes Cases

Another way girls show their style is through clothing — what style they choose is a reflection of who they are. The girls surveyed told us what they consider to be their own personal clothing style. And to give us a little more insight into who they are, they revealed their favorite outfits.

Trendy is tops when it comes to style choices — more girls called their style "in" and "now" than any other clothing description. But comfort is also key, we learned. **Here's a look at the top styles:**

- Trendy/Hip/In   (31%)
- Comfortable   (21%)
- Preppy   (12%)

- Cool (12%)
- Casual (8%)
- Stylish (6%)
- Unique (6%)

Even though it probably changes pretty often, everyone has a favorite outfit of the moment — one you wish you could wear every day. The girls surveyed gave us an inside peek at the stars of their closets. **Here are some descriptions of what they love wearing. No doubt you'll be able to tell a little about each as she reveals her top choice:**

"My black pair of board shorts with a light blue tank top and comfy sandals."
    — **Heather,** 13, East Stroudsburg, Pennsylvania

"My new A&F wind suit pants, which are navy with a red-and-white stripe down each leg. They tie at the waist, so I wear a white Guess halter top and show my stomach. And I wear a cool silver belly chain."
    — **Christie,** 15, Marion, Arkansas

"My Lucky brand blue jeans and Tommy Hilfiger shirt."
    — **Christi,** 15, Franklin, Kentucky

"Baggy pants and a short shirt."
    — **Shanika,** 10, Hartford, Alabama

"A tank top with sandals and jean shorts."
    — **M.,** 11, Oswego, Illinois

"A skirt like the one Britney wears in the video for 'Baby One More Time' and a white baby-doll tank."
    — **Mahleea,** 11, Lawrence, Kansas

"Flare jeans and a long-sleeve baby blue shirt."
    — **Jenny,** 13, Buffalo Grove, Illinois

"Cargo pants and a white T-shirt with a shirt over it."
    — **Elizabeth,** 14, DeMotte, Indiana

"Blue overalls and a spaghetti strap shirt with white flowers."
    — **Nicole,** 13, Henderson, Nevada

"Bright orange board shorts and a dark blue spaghetti-strap T with a big flower in the top left corner and a small flower in the bottom right corner."
    — **Kelly,** 13, Gold Hill, Oregon

Chapter Six

Celeb Stats

The results are in! The girls surveyed spoke out about who they thought were the hottest stars around, and the Backstreet Boys came out on top. These guys popped up everywhere, only to be outdone by a female celeb in the all-time-fave-celeb category. And who would that be? Drew Barrymore, star of the all-time fave flick *Ever After*. Take a peek at the top celeb picks in just about every category!

All-Time Favorite Celebrity

Drew's definitely got it! The girl who got her start in *E.T.* is the number one fave celeb according to our survey. And you don't have to be a Backstreet Boy to be the top guy in this category — just ask funny guy Adam Sandler. **The top five are:**

1) Drew Barrymore
2) Adam Sandler
3) Justin Timberlake (of 'N Sync)
4) Nick Carter (of Backstreet Boys)
5) Sarah Michelle Gellar

Favorite Actor

What was Gwyneth thinking, getting rid of the hottest guy on the big screen? Ben's a winner, that's for sure. Mr. All-American, Will Smith, also proved that he's a star with super staying power. **Here's who the girls we surveyed named as their fave male actors:**

1) Ben Affleck
2) Will Smith
3) Ryan Phillipe
4) Adam Sandler
5) Matt Damon
6) James Van Der Beek
7) Freddie Prinze Jr.

Favorite Actress

Yup, you guessed it — Drew's number one in this category, too! **Here are the top actresses of the big and little screens according to our survey:**

1) Drew Barrymore
2) Jennifer Love Hewitt
3) Sarah Michelle Gellar
4) Julia Roberts
5) Neve Campbell
6) Sandra Bullock
7) Brandy

Your Favorite Movie

Can Drew do no wrong? Her movie topped the list of fave flicks.

The top movie choice is:

1) *Ever After*

Honorable mentions are:

2) *Grease*
3) *Hope Floats*
4) *I Know What You Did Last Summer*
5) *Liar, Liar*
6) *The Parent Trap*

Flick Picks: Films You've Just Gotta See at Least Once

Make your next get-together a movie night by renting one of the following films you and your friends are guaranteed to enjoy!

Anastasia: Talk about a troubled teen! Meg Ryan provides the voice for this animated tale of a girl in search of her true identity.

Attack of the Killer Tomatoes!: A cheesy, low-budget horror spoof about a really big vegetable. It's way more goofy than scary. Can't find the original? Look for the sequels, Return of the Killer Tomatoes (starring George Clooney) and Killer Tomatoes Eat France!

Babe: A hilarious and sweet story of a cute pig learning to be a sheepherder.

Back to the Future: Michael J. Fox makes this time-travel tale a true adventure.

Beetlejuice: This slightly twisted flick features one of star Winona Ryder's first movie appearances.

Dead Poets Society: Robin Williams and a cast of cuties help make this movie set at a private boys' school one that you won't soon forget.

Father of the Bride: A not-too-mushy tale that any girl who's the apple of her father's eye will adore.

George of the Jungle: Who cares if it's a little on the silly side — Brendan Fraser is absolutely adorable in the starring role.

Sleepless in Seattle: Get the tissues out — this tear-jerking love story starring Meg Ryan and Tom Hanks will move even the most reluctant romantic.

The *Star Wars* Series: Before there was Episode I, there were Episodes IV, V, and VI (odd as that may seem). *Star Wars, The Empire Strikes Back,* and *Return of the Jedi* are some of the best sci-fi films ever made, so if you haven't seen 'em, check them out.

Willy Wonka and the Chocolate Factory: You have to see this movie at least once in your life — it's silly, funny, and it'll make your mouth water!

Favorite Music Group

The BSBs really rock your world. This boy band is so hot, they nearly blew everyone else off the charts. Everyone, that is, except for 'N Sync, whose songs and singers you just love. **The top three fave groups are:**

1) Backstreet Boys
2) 'N Sync
3) TLC

Favorite Male Musician/Singer

Everybody's going *loco* for Ricky . . . and we have a suspicion it's not just his voice that drives you crazy! **The top five male singers are:**

1) Ricky Martin
2) Justin Timberlake (of 'N Sync)
3) Usher
4) Nick Carter (of Backstreet Boys)
5) Brian Littrell (of Backstreet Boys)

Favorite Female Musician/Singer

Oh, baby — Britney is the best female singer around according to our survey. But while her first album was a huge chart-topper, let's just hope she can do it one more time! **The top five female singers are:**

1) Britney Spears
2) Brandy
3) Shania Twain
4) Mariah Carey
5) Jewel, Sarah McLachlan (tie)

Favorite Athlete

No bull here: Michael Jordan is a superstar athlete in your eyes. Even though he's retired, his legend lives on! Girl athletes also made their way onto the list, with skater Tara Lipinski and soccer star Mia Hamm beating out other male athletes to take home the bronze medal in this category. **The top three fave athletes are:**

1) Michael Jordan
2) Brett Favre
3) Tara Lipinski, Mia Hamm (tie)

Your Favorite Show on the Tube

From the looks of it, Pacey, Dawson, Joey, Jen, and the rest of the *Dawson's Creek* characters have really captured girls' hearts! This drama took top honors in the TV category. **The favorite TV shows are:**

1) *Dawson's Creek*
2) *Friends*
3) *Buffy the Vampire Slayer*
4) *7th Heaven*
5) *Boy Meets World*
6) MTV's *Total Request Live*

Cutest Male Celebrity

The girls we heard from voted Nick Carter of the Backstreet Boys the number one cutest celeb around — by far! **Other cute celebs that got honorable mentions are:**

2) Ben Affleck
3) Justin Timberlake
4) Freddie Prinze Jr.
5) Ryan Phillipe

Best-Looking Female Celebrity

Mirror, mirror, on the wall . . . looks like Brandy is the fairest of them all! **Top three votes for the prettiest female celeb went to:**

1) Brandy
2) Sarah Michelle Gellar
3) Jennifer Love Hewitt

Chapter Seven

Oh, Boys

Funny how things change . . . most likely, not long ago you wanted nothing to do with boys. Blech — what jerks! But now that you are no longer a little kid, we bet your feelings about boys are changing. Nearly every girl we heard from (98%) confessed that she has had a crush on a boy at one time or another. Read on to find out how girls like you feel about boys.

The Best Kinds of Boys

When we asked the girls surveyed to tell us what kind of boys they like, the answers really varied — but one thing's for sure, most of you like 'em cute and nice! **The kinds of boys the girls surveyed like are:**

1) Cute
2) Nice
3) Funny
4) Smart
5) Sweet
6) Caring
7) Athletic/sporty
8) Trusting
9) Popular

Boy Types: Can You Spot Yours?

What's your ultimate boy like? Is he the sporty type, the jokester, or the boy next door? It can be difficult to identify all the different boy types out there, so to help, here's a look at a few types you're likely to encounter:

✳ **The Jokester:** He has a quick, off-the-wall comment for everything you say. Sometimes his oddball ways can make others think he's a little *loco*, but deep down he's as sweet as can be.

How to spot him: He'll be the one always getting into trouble for goofing off.

What he'll be wearing: A Beavis and Butt-head T-shirt.

Why you'll like him: You won't be able to stop laughing.

What he'll need to work on: Stopping with the jokes long enough to get serious every now and then.

The girl for him: Definitely has a great sense of humor. Though his jokes are usually harmless, she has to have thick skin to put up with all the teasing.

❋ **The Sportster:** This is the guy who plays practically every single sport your school or town offers. Sure, he takes the occasional break to do homework and eat a huge meal, but the sporty boy would rather be out on the field than anywhere else.

How to spot him: Notice that ball whizzing over your head? Follow it to its source and you're likely to find a sportster.

What he'll be wearing: A baseball cap and his fave team's jersey.

Why you'll like him: It'll be a blast to cheer him on to victory.

What he'll need to work on: Stop watching replays of every last game on ESPN 24/7 and do something you wanna do for a change!

The girl for him: She'll either be an athlete herself or will love to watch sports. Having common interests makes any friendship stronger.

✳ **The Boy Next Door:** Usually a charmer, the boy next door is loved by just about everyone. He's so sweet, though, that sometimes girls tend to overlook him as crush material.

How to spot him: He'll be the one helping some sweet elderly lady with her groceries.

What he'll be wearing: Jeans and a T-shirt — of course.

Why you'll like him: How can you resist? This boy is so nice that, if nothing else, you'll want him as a best bud.

What he'll need to work on: He might just spend more time chatting with your mom and dad than with you.

The girl for him: Sweet just like him, but also well-rounded and happy.

✳ **The Bookworm:** Somewhere out there is the next Bill Gates . . . and he just might be sitting next to you in class. Don't discount the boy who's buried beneath that stack of books — he could be a future tycoon.

How to spot him: He'll have the coolest gadgets — like an electronic address book or a watch that does everything.

What he'll be wearing: This boy couldn't care less about what he's got on.

Why you'll like him: He'll challenge you mentally.

> *What he'll need to work on:* Sometimes people who are book-smart can be lacking in the people-skills category. It may take some coaching to get him out of his social shell.
>
> *The girl for him:* Someone who's supersocial might be just the right type to get this boy away from his computer screen every now and then.

Making the First Move

Most girls we surveyed don't believe in the old-fashioned concept that it's the guys who should do the asking out. Ninety percent think it's perfectly fine for a girl to ask a boy out! It's good to know that times have changed and things are more equal now. As 13-year-old Heather from Pennsylvania puts it: *"We're not living in the 70s anymore!"*

Datin' Time

A crush is one thing, but actually going out with a boy (gulp!) is a totally different story. Most girls feel that it's okay to start dating at around age 14.

Conclusion

Thoughts to Treasure

You and your friends may be young, but that doesn't stop you from having a great deal of wisdom and insight. Your very cool viewpoints are proof of that, as are the words you shared with us. **When asked what their favorite poem, saying, or quote was, here are some of the words that the girls we surveyed said they lived by:**

"'Shoot for the moon and you'll clearly be among the stars,' and 'Today is the tomorrow we worried about yesterday. Was it worth it?'"
— **Nancy,** 14, Macon, Georgia

"You gotta get a little bit more oomph on it!"
— **Haley,** 10, Leechburg, Pennsylvania

"Live life to its fullest."
— **Lindsey,** 15, Pennsylvania

"Give people more than they expect and do it cheerfully. Learn the rules and then break some."
— **Maria,** San Jose, California

"Cross your bridges when you come to them."
 — **M.**, 11, Oswego, Illinois

"Speak when you are angry and you'll make the best speech you ever regret."
 — **Anonymous**, 13

By now you've learned a lot about other girls who are around your age. And hopefully you've learned a little about yourself as well — how alike you are to other girls as well as how different and unique you are compared to them. One thing's certain — girls today are pretty cool! Not only do you have the courage to speak your mind about tons of stuff, but you also have some pretty admirable views on things and seem to have your heads on straight. That's girl power for you!

The *Get Real!* Survey

Your age:

Your first name (optional):

Your last name (optional):

Your hometown (city and state):

You and Your World

1) How would you describe yourself in one word?

2) Who are your role models?

3) If you could change one thing about yourself — not related to your appearance — what would it be?

4) If you could change one thing about your appearance, what would it be?

5) Something that makes you really happy is:

6) Something that makes you really sad is:

7) What scares you the most?

8) What has been your most embarrassing moment?

9) The scariest thing that ever happened to you was:

10) The worst thing you ever did was:

11) Do you believe in God?

12) Do you attend church or a synagogue regularly? If so, how often?

13) Do you have a favorite poem, saying, or quote? If so, what is it?

14) Where do you see yourself in 15–20 years?

Your Family and Your Friends

1) Who do you live with? Check one:
     ___ Both parents plus one or more siblings (brothers and/or sisters)
     ___ Both parents
     ___ Mom only
     ___ Dad only
     ___ Grandparent(s)
     ___ Other (please explain)
     ___ Are you happy with your current living situation? Please explain:

2) Have you ever lied to your parents? If so, what about?

3) What's your biggest gripe about your parents?

4) What's the worst trouble you've ever been in with your parents?

5) Do your parents ever give you a hard time about (check all that apply):
___ Your choice of friends?
___ Your hairstyle?
___ The clothes you wear?
___ Wearing makeup?
___ Talking on the phone too much?
___ Not spending enough time on schoolwork?
___ Staying out too late?
___ Not doing your chores?
___ Your room being a mess?
___ Other (please explain):

6) Do you have any brothers? If yes, tell us how many and how old they are.

7) Do you have any sisters? If yes, tell us how many and how old they are.

8) If you have sisters, what do you most often fight about?

9) Have you ever snitched on a sibling (brother or sister)? If so, 'fess up and tell us about it:

10) Do you have a pet? If so, list the kind of animal you have and his/her name:

11) What qualities do you look for in a good friend?

12) What do you and your friends like to do for fun?

13) Tell us about your best friend(s) (How long have you been friends, why do you think she's the greatest, describe her in one word, etc.):

14) How much time do you spend a week:

Talking on the phone with your friends?

Writing e-mails to friends?

Hanging out with your friends?

15) Have you ever revealed a secret to someone else that a friend entrusted to you? If so, what was the secret and what happened as a result of you spilling the beans?

16) Has a friend ever revealed one of your secrets? Please explain:

17) Have you ever snitched on a friend? If so, give us the details:

School

1) Which class do you just love (OK, so maybe you just like it a lot)?

2) What would you say are the top problems at *your* school? (Number them from one to three, with one being the biggest problem.)

___ Alcohol abuse
___ Lack of moral values
___ Gangs
___ Kids with too many family problems
___ Smoking
___ Peer pressure
___ Grades/poor scholastic achievement
___ Lack of parental involvement
___ Other (please explain)

3) Which class do you wish would go away forever?

4) Have you ever cheated on a test? If so, please explain:

5) Have you ever cheated on an assignment? If so, please explain:

6) Have you ever skipped school (ditched)? If so, why — what did you do instead?

7) Do you ever pass notes during class? If so, have you ever been caught?

8) What's the worst trouble you've ever been in at school?

9) Have you ever given a teacher a false excuse as to why you didn't complete an assignment (like, your dog ate your homework)? If so, do tell:

10) Does your school have a dress code or do you wear uniforms? If so, what are your uniforms like?

11) Do you think uniforms are a good idea? Why or why not?

Fun and Leisure Time

1) How do you like to spend your free time? (Check all that apply)
    ___ Playing sports
    ___ In school clubs
    ___ Hanging out with friends
    ___ Watching TV
    ___ Reading books
    ___ Reading magazines
    ___ Listening to music
    ___ Writing letters or e-mail
    ___ Shopping
    ___ Playing video or CD-ROM games
    ___ At the mall
    ___ Talking on the phone
    ___ Other:

2) What is your number one hobby?

3) What are your favorite types of books to read? (Check all that apply.)

    ____ Books about celebrities (actors, musicians, etc.)
    ____ Historical fiction
    ____ Fashion and beauty books
    ____ Romantic fiction
    ____ Biographies of famous people in history
    ____ Books about athletes
    ____ Thrillers, mysteries or suspense books
    ____ Adventure books
    ____ Science fiction
    ____ Books about animals
    ____ Other (please explain):

4) Describe the best vacation you ever took:

5) Describe the worst vacation you ever took:

6) Do you play sports? If so, which ones?

7) What is your favorite sport to play?

8) What is your favorite sport to watch?

9) Do you have your own e-mail account? If not, do you share one with someone else (family)? Please explain:

10) How much time do you spend "surfing" the Net?

11) Tell us about your room (Color, how it's decorated/organized, what you have on your walls, etc.):

12) How would you describe your clothing style?

13) Describe your favorite outfit:

Celebs and Stuff

1) Your all-time favorite celebrity is:

2) Your favorite actor is:

3) Your favorite actress is:

4) Your all-time favorite movie is:

5) Your favorite music group is:

6) Your favorite male musician/singer is:

7) Your favorite female musician/singer is:

8) Your favorite athlete is:

9) Your favorite TV show is:

10) The cutest male celebrity is:

11) The prettiest female celebrity is:

Boys

1) Have you ever had a crush on someone?

2) What kind of boys do you like?

3) Do you think it's OK for a girl to ask a boy out?

4) At what age do you think it's OK to start dating?

Choices, Choices

Please select one choice for each question:

1) When you think of your future, do you see yourself:
___ Living in a big city?
___ Living in a small town?

2) Which of the following is more important for you to have?
___ A great career
___ A great family

3) Would you rather have a life where you:
___ Are able to travel the world
___ Have a nice, stable home
___ Make lots of money
___ Have a job you love

4) Would you rather be:
____ Good-looking?
____ Smart?

5) Would you rather go out with a guy who was:
____ Good-looking?
____ Smart?

○